EMILY DICKINSON'S LEXICON

Poems

KATIE LEHMAN

DOS MADRES

2023

DOS MADRES PRESS INC.
P.O. Box 294, Loveland, Ohio 45140
www.dosmadres.com   editor@dosmadres.com

Dos Madres is dedicated to the belief that the small press is essential
to the vitality of contemporary literature as a carrier of the new voice,
as well as the older, sometimes forgotten voices of the past. And in an
ever more virtual world, to the creation of fine books pleasing to the
eye and hand.

Dos Madres is named in honor of Vera Murphy and Libbie Hughes,
the "Dos Madres" whose contributions have made this press possible.

Dos Madres Press, Inc. is an Ohio Not For Profit Corporation and a
501 (c) (3) qualified public charity. Contributions are tax deductible.

Executive Editor: Robert J. Murphy

Illustration & Book Design: Elizabeth H. Murphy
www.illusionstudios.net

Cover art: Rachel Lapp Whitt. Based on the Dickinson daguerreotype
held in the Amherst College Archives and Special Collections. Detail
of recreated floral wallpaper in the wings of butterfly and bird and in
the envelope based on original fragments found in Emily Dickinson's
bedroom. Design by Marylou Davis, courtesy of the Emily Dickinson
Museum.

Typeset in Adobe Garamond Pro & Baskerville Old Face
ISBN 978-1-953252-88-3
Library of Congress Control Number: 2023941676

First Edition

Published by Dos Madres Press, Inc.

ACKNOWLEDGMENTS

Grateful acknowledgment is given to the following journals in which some of the poems first appeared, often in earlier forms: *The Fortnightly Review:* "And Her Herbarium," "By the Pier, an Island," "Called Back," "Emily Dickinson's Lexicon," "Evogram," "Her Daguerreotype," "Monarch," "Now Horses," "Picture in a Pandemic," "Poetry Cloak," "Reverie," "Sleepy Tom," "Virgil's Font"; *GilChrist Letter:* "Seeing the Deer"; *Great River Review:* "Afternoon Tea"; *JAMA:* "Oxheart"; *Journal of the Center for Mennonite Writing:* "The Fields," "Garden Talk," "Poem for the Gardener," "Rain in the Garden"; *Notre Dame Review:* "American History Primer," "Bon Secours," "Night Eye," "Piano Lesson."

GRATITUDE

My gratitude goes to my family, Marlon and Finn, for their constant love and for keeping me grounded in "real life"; and to my parents, who instilled in me at a young age the importance of an imaginative mind and a compassionate heart. I also thank my cousin Rebecca Crotty for her lifelong friendship.

I thank Denis Boyles, managing editor of *The Fortnightly Review,* and Robert Murphy, executive editor of Dos Madres Press, for believing in my work, and Elizabeth Murphy for her artistry in book design.

I thank Rachel Lapp Whitt for the book's cover art, as well as for her fierce empathy, brave spirit, and sense for justice in this world.

My appreciation also goes to my many teachers along the way: at Notre Dame, John Matthias, whose work makes me write better poems and whose guidance has been invaluable; and Sonia Gernes for her enduring friendship and example; at Goshen College, the late John Fisher who taught me the art of revision and in so doing helped shape my poetic voice—I only wish I could show him this book. I also thank John Fisher and his wife Pauline for introducing me to Ireland in the summer of 1993. I thank Don Lawrence Troyer, MD, who steadied my boat many times over; Brother Martin Dally, O.S.B., for his compassion and kinship so many years ago; the late Joel Elkes, physician and painter, for seeing light in me when I could not (he used the Hebrew word *nephesh*); the late Sister Benedict O'Beirne, O.S.B., about whom many of these poems are written; and Jeannine Yeager, my childhood piano teacher, who turned my ear to music. Finally, I am forever indebted to David K. Williams, who lit the spark. This book is dedicated to him with deepest gratitude and love.

for David K. Williams

I reckon – When I count at all –
First – Poets – Then the Sun –

—Emily Dickinson

TABLE OF CONTENTS

EMILY DICKINSON'S LEXICON

Her Daguerreotype

Just prior to her portrait sitting she stood next to the damask
drapery, hem to hem, with its back layers of muslin and dimity

to let in the sun, while the eager Mount Holyoke daguerreotypist
immersed himself in the theatrics of setting up his camera obscura

in all its myriad parts: leveling stand, copper plates coated on
the face with silver nitrate, iodine and bromide boxes, cabinet

and clamps. Until his two arms with one gesture signal Emily
to the unseen chair. Her bold chestnut burr hair is pinned back,

her subtly plump hands with long narrowing fingers that crossed
the laced ribbon around her neck just an hour before now clasp

the flowers she had turned quickly back to pick; her light-glancing
eye had caught sight of them on her way there. Shoulders angling

down: her right arm, with inch-wide cuffs, baroque tablecloth,
a book, a Bible? form a still life with disembodied hand—Is that

her finest brocade? Did she speak, smile? Her lips do not say
in the absence of not just hers but all 19th-century teeth. How

long did her erudite gaze linger in ambient light before her
image over blue mercury flame materialized on a plate

that would otherwise be a mirror? before her likeness—her
sherry-colored eyes, her wren-sized frame, as she wrote to

Higginson—imprinted on history? But this is 1847, before
she lost a world or felt a funeral in her brain. Though a fixed

melancholy has set in. At home on North Pleasant her bureau
is yet devoid of poetry, the forty fascicles bound with string—

but holds one green-bound herbarium in which she has
already decided to press the pansies with loosestrife stem.

Monarch

Cyclical and sparse, her eyelid-thin wings approach
and disapproach among the grasses. Unassuming,
she only covets what she knows: a single worn reed
of herself, dark covert, uncoaxable as the worm

she once was. Before the white-spotted wings,
before the stained-glass veins. Idling brown earth
at close measure. Closer at length, but she knows
closeness is not her answer. If it is a loveliness

she feels or a kind of loneliness, only the husbandry
of tears will make her radiance known. How her
cautious love perplexes the moth who darts
unblinkingly into the porch light. Filamental,

she is compatible to late dusk or perceivable grief.
Admonish, and she's gone—yet I conspire she longs
for earth's untiring clasp, longs even, all preconceptions
removed—to lay her orange and black chivalry down.

January Calf

Brash iceberg, you were
calved too soon—rippled skin,
hide of sewn linen, licked
of vein strokes, a raw weep

and blemish. What packed
hemisphere pushed you out
in this southern, sudden slip
of a rope and pulled me in

so tight? Pitched were pieces,
pierces like clamor and glass
crashing. Clamped in an earache—
I thought a nest of baby birds

had fallen from the barn eaves'
wooden claws. January calf, size
of an infant human, I wrapped
a vinyl apron, soiled with

teat dip and cow dung round your
rashing, gum-stuck body. The slight
weight across my shoulder plunged
me under the metal feed bunk rails,

over the leaning bale-tied gates,
while you yelped, straining
for some other mother or
cover. A barn door, open

harbor, gray and sliding, banged wildly,
wind-swept and rain amuck. Inside the
heat lamps pulsated, scratchy bulbs,
the milk pump kicked and thumped,

where I had laid you, seal-like, in one
chaotic crib of straw. Cobweb lint and
spider stalk, you slept, died, wombless,
the kittens all afluff on your back.

Eulogy before Death

Kylemore Abbey, Connemara, Co. Galway, Ireland

I

Because I cannot
tell you then—
I say your eulogy

before your death,
preferring this
to something polite,

something Christian
like *She was ready to go*
to Our Lord in Heaven.

And even though
I will believe it I won't,
as I don't now

in thinking about it.
And why should I
think about it when

you are awake, up
before the others, alone
and unlit, praying in

the chapel. Still tiring about
the farm with a broken pitch-
fork, sifting silage, felling

feed pellets to hens and pullets,
filling water barrels and buckets
in their corrugated tenements.

Still slapping creamed
butter with wooden paddles,
slap slap clack, as you pummel

the large, salted yellow mass
into one-pound rectangles.
Sliding the roller across and

this way back, distilling
the water out. Two arms
agitating a milky marrow, one

and then the other, rowing
the churning oar over. One arm,
broken by a fresh heifer,

healed wrong, but naturally,
the other stitched back on
after you drove off the road's

shoulder into a ditch. They
made you go to hospital then,
and you let them, befriending

the young nurse who dared
to ask you: "Tell me, Sister,
what *is* it like to be a nun?"

II

And tell *me,* what if
there are no cows in heaven,
what if there are no fields

to walk in, to account for each
suckler and check for early
springing? Surely you will not

want to go then. Surely you will not
leave the blackberries, throbbing
all bruised purple and wasping

in their thorn-corseted thickets,
unpicked the year you die. And the
wine-red currants you operated on

like your surgeon uncle, incising
the soil, a low hummock of earth-
tissue and tomb-suture,

reassuring the thin, stitch-veins,
transplanting them to the farm.
And the poor fig tree who bore

only five figs in two years and
the parsley sprouting green lace—
all over—a silver newness, a turn

of solace, a pallor, will wonder
why you didn't come
after tea today. And the kettle

will be cold on the stove, in stupor.
And the apples and the crabapples,
doddering patient, sweetened in

boiling water and granular sugar,
the jelly sapping itself down
the plate and still not ready—

The other nuns, unaware, will surely sell
Mrs. Barrett then, the way she could
corner, not cower, like any good bull

and who made us laugh, suspicious
of Mad Cow Disease. And
Blue Fairy, scant milker,

they are sure to sell her, not knowing
she wandered, starving,
into your fields' wide stretch

of November pasture, eating only
the bitter crabgrass the bold sheep left.
And who will milk the cows

when the procession of black robes
walks with bent heads over split
hymnals to the Gothic cemetery

where slim, basalt crosses
peep out like Ohio grackles in
winter from the ice-glittering stones?

III

You will be
gathering pails and
looping yellow and light blue

bale ties around your fingers
and into your denim apron pocket.
You will be walking the makeshift

fences that dangle with frazzled
strands of the same ties, leaving no
hole for the sheep to get through,

cheating with stolen grass—
Your cell will still be locked
Sister Benedict—

like when you went to America
not knowing you'd come back with
your brother's ashes. You said

at his funeral a marching band
was practicing across the street
and its music came in and

sprang up when the priest, lifting
his hands, said, "Let us Pray"—
and on cue the cymbals clashed

and the lofty tone notes, *Santa Claus
is coming to town* resounded through
the brassy church conclave and

made you remember him the way
he would have wanted it. So I suppose
you will be hovering

in the alder bush and pulpwood,
marking time in disguise of
a ferric chaffinch, and your song

will lift your ash-wings, rising
like a heron would, with her long,
blue-gray and pen-slim legs. But

they, the others, will have no one
to tell them it would have been
three years since the blue heron

appeared in its full grandeur
in the garden lush, a hush—then
a patter, a flutter of two wings aflight. So

you will need to appear in
the fullness of December, in
the splendor of the holly trees,

dappling in hard berries, red
against leaf-hearts of green
and limb-wood, flaming drops

of orange with the docile streams,
making the mountains speak,
beckoning you back to them.

And the land, loyal land, that
walked beside you all the long while
of your life, will tell you

its secret then, how it longed
for your prayer to be translated
into a language it could begin

to understand. And you will
tell each named field and
let them be grazed on days

they should be worked in.
And the calves—tell them
not to worry, feed

the sick ones store-bought
Quaker Oats, stirring the
speckled sawdust flakes

into mush and milk. Tell them
they must eat it they must
get better, only because you

would want it so much. Only because
that is what you would have wanted
any sick creature to have. And if

any creature was sick enough to
die, surely you would dignify its
death by telling everything about it.

IV

Like Bran, your waning
border collie mix you buried
beneath the kitchen window

where she had lain all the last year
of her life. Like the wallowing chestnut
hen, stumbling absent. You held her

esophagated rope-of-a-neck and twisted
the air shaft shut, out of misery. Like the
cedar fox, still uncaught, that made you

so cross, tracing tufts of orange feather
and white under-fluff where the struggle
had been, without one bantam hen

or chick left. And if you had a gun
you would have shot him if
he hadn't been so hungry. And like

Sonny, your handsome Charolais,
you had to send to slaughter.
And when the men came and lured

him onto the lorry, you came into
the farm kitchen and couldn't watch
and couldn't cry. And

whenever I do I hear your voice
inside me, *Don't cry*, and I do
and you let me, knowing

it's good to cry. And you
do cry too. And Sonny, he
tore his scrotum on a barbed wire—

we found it dangling on a rusted thorn,
ashamed in the hidden brambles. But
you said words that didn't have to

hide themselves, didn't have to feel
ashamed. Nothing was embarrassing
enough not to be said. So I say

your eulogy before your death.
I say it only because I don't want it
so much. But when you do, tell me,

what prayer do I pray? Tell me,
in what fierce field will I find
your blazingly gentle life veiled in?

(i.m. Sr. Benedict O'Beirne, O.S.B.,
1928–2018)

14

Thoreau's Sisters

Why hadn't I heard of either of them?
        Helen and Sophia—in daguerreotypes
they share the same pressed lips as their famous
        brother, a distinctly Thoreau nose.

Sophia, an artist (it is *her* sketch that serves as
        frontispiece to *Walden*), amateur botanist,
amanuensis, an editor with a sense for business
        (and it was *she,* not pencilmaker

Henry David Thoreau, who managed
        their father's factory after his death),
and, not least, being only two years younger,
        Henry's ever-loyal companion. In true

sisterly form, Sophia brought food to Henry
        that first night he went to the woods, to his
cabin at Walden (though, *he didn't like to receive it very
        well,* having *just* begun his experiment).

Helen was cerebral, a staunch antislavery
        activist, friend to Frederick Douglass.
The two sisters together went to the Anti-Slavery
        Convention in Boston (Henry was out

measuring Concord to Mt. Monadnock to
        Mt. Greylock). Henry's *moral lodestar,*
taking social injustice to heart, Helen was sympathetic
        to her eccentric brother. With

Emily Dickinson stealth she refused
        churchgoing—where slaveholders sat
and women were not permitted to speak—
        to her dying day. When it was

only Sophia and Henry left, the pair
        became sole confidants, climbed
Nashawtuc to observe phoebe and chickadee
        and jay. While sauntering through

southwest meadows Henry would tuck
        plant specimens in the handsewn
pocket of his botany hat (of course he'd have
        a botany hat!) for Sophia—

and when on his deathbed Henry asked
        for playing children, Sophia promptly
found playing children. After his death,
        she'd inscribe her brother's poems

on Shagbark Hickory leaves—as he had done.
        And it was Sophia who deciphered
Henry's messy handwriting across his papers
        and manuscripts; his illegible *Journal*

perplexes present-day scientists, but she'd be
        able to discern the first flowering dates
of the 500 wildflower species Henry tracked. And
        despite male counterparts taking credit

for her meticulous work, Sophia alone
        edited many of Thoreau's posthumous
publications. Though she was quickly dismissed
        by early biographers as being *more fanatical*

than wise in her editorial presumptions; fussy with
        "adverse reactions"—*crotchety;* having
to be *handled carefully* in her brother's loss, in
        her seemingly endless weeping.

Garden Talk

Victorian Walled Garden, Kylemore Abbey, Ireland

Sunlit, the vegetation lifts
after a rain that doused every leaf
low on its stem. Mist and tome, it is
another's secret, an old solemnity
in which we walk. Our boots talk, taking to
the grassy squeak, the yellow wet. What

quickening speaks in such respite? The rain barrel
full, it seeps its orange-flaked ridge
over. But who owns it? Our eyes in a pale pleasure of lisp or gasp
are painless. The water pock, the pock-drip,
the upraised parsley beds that sift a soil specked with white.
All is quietly kept in our seeing.

Now the orchard's in our keeping. And a trellis
above the garden gate hangs above all that is
growing, light and green. Your hands grasp
gray limbs, a slip of bark. *It's possible, maybe—*
you say you're too old for this, climb
anyway, I stay behind—squinting light, black lash,

apples. *What Autumn awoke*
attentive, on a sudden leaf?
We think we hear ladies drinking their mid-morning tea.
You almost—the swishing of skirts, as they walk.
Hurry and *hurry.*
A branch brush, a hush, a balmy clutch—

What talk surmises them now? What heaven
gave in within the ten-foot
drop? We step, cautious not

to disturb it—plateaus of iron, rhododendron
silk and brick, berry thick, a prick of needle bush. *Don't go and
why so soon? We've hardly met.* Our

breath in the swallow of others' loveliness is
unguarded, a joyous whimper in the trees.
We decipher this year's crop is—*Taste,
just as sweet*—idling in, a
plenitude, sworn by the oak, the grazing
of many, and us turning the latch lock out.

Emily Dickinson's Lexicon

The Way I read a Letter's—this—
'Tis first—I lock the Door—
And push it with my fingers—next—
For transport it be sure—

—Emily Dickinson

Her *Collected* has the *weight* of a *Bible,*
    although more *kind,* but just as
scrupulous, its binding now un*thread.* Not so
        clear as to *exclude*; anyone can *find*

oneself within, its *compassion all*-encompassing.
        Hedge, heed, heel. Her cautionary *poem*
of what *suffering* can *incur,* or *Joy* reflect. *Stone, bee,*
        riding the rails, *hurl, hurrah,* through *Eternity*—`

but also here with me—at *eighteen*—as I *knock* and
        from a *window* a caretaker (though *grimly*)
perceives, opens at *bent arm's length,* and (from
        the *tilt* of my *head)*—at a *Slant*—

the Amherst Homestead's *back door.* (The museum
        is *closed,* she *asserts, dissuading* me.) Though
sighing, seeing from the *stoop,* my drawn-down *face,*
        my *silent plea*—she succumbs, then *reluctantly*

lets me in. We *climb* the *narrow wooden stair* as
        it *cracks* like a misaligned spine beneath us
to the *white dress, white* counterpane on *bed.* How many
        letters did Emily un*seal* (or poems on

envelopes *press)* in this *room,* having *locked* the *Door*—
         their *transport sure.* I am voyeur (she did not
use "voyeur")—she did not use "permeate" or
         "imbue." But I *take* my *Book* and take—

along with the *Bird* that *did not know,* the *Wind*
         that did not *require the Grass to answer,* as
well as the *Brave Bobolink*—all the *clovers*—and
         one following Daisy folded inside its *pages.*

20

The Apple Cutting

Connemara, Co. Galway, Ireland

Before they come to cut the orchard down,
      we fill up box crates and buckets
with apples, as many as we can reach or
      shake down. A reversed pageantry,
private and resolute, bestows us in earnest

up to the leaf-bunched branches. Hence
      a crop of hard and benevolent bulbs—
softly lit and lightly blushed, pale red, orange haze;
      each a robin's oxidized breast. We start
storing, after filling the garden shed, the surplus

in dirt-burrowed mounds. How like a burial
      the orchard then is. Like bouquets
we place fresh stems on the apples' graves and
      daily tend. At night the badgers
smell a rotting pulp, leave half-eaten rinds

on a dew-wet path. By morning we cover over,
      hear the branches' crooked severing,
the scream of the heightening saw, see
      the carnage of leaves drying, a
scattering of securer apples, once unreachable,

underneath us now. Inverted, the trunks turn
      their dull claws over. Prehistoric, they
are themselves the birds who stepped
      from the sea. How long the trees
here breathed, clutched in a planetary vice.

We mean to go back, to retrieve the ones we
have buried. But if we forget, our
efforts will be kept by earth-darting robins
carrying to their far oak's nest
sprigs from a grove burgeoning with seeds.

Evogram

Being different is not an illness.

—Greta Thunberg

My son at seven is afraid of water, the slightest drop
on his arm. I tell him he was born from water, smallest
amniote, floating weightless within a fluid-filled globe,
gravid in the illuminated dark, his lungs yet to form

like the primeval fish he once was. But he is more specific:
it was Tiktaalik, the earliest known land vertebrate in
the Carboniferous. Lobe-finned, a pioneer amphibian
with limbs. I suggest he is the fishlike ostracoderm

with intricate armored skin. But the classification is
outdated, the metaphor has holes—and he swims. It
is the differentiation, that spate of rain uncommitted
to pools that startles and darts then makes wet. "Ouch,"

he says from welts cropping up like a pox on his sleeve.
He's become afraid of fiction. Of dramatic tension, or
an image on a classmate's page. Stick to the scientific,
the facts: All birds descend from dinosaurs, not the

bird-hipped Ornithischians (nonavian, he reminds me)
but the lizard-hipped Saurischians, in an evolutionary
twist of plot. Not the Sauropods but the Theropods. Long
before birds emerged in their brightly colored cacophony,

Archaeopteryx—Old Wing—appeared in its primitive plumage.
I look up "Theropod": Tyrannosaurus Rex—Tyrant Lizard
King. I think: What mammal hid among the late Cretacean
forest?—and then: What fear followed him here on this

Quaternary evening, under these trees, below this sky?
what predator or prey? Like him, I grasp for definitions
and the labels they name: *fixation on particular subjects;
problems with processing physical sensations.* But something

primordial halts my breath: *We are individuals after all—*
what tricks the brain plays, what convergences of light
bore at the truth of things. I glance from my text—
he runs among the rasping of wings in the garden.

Piano Lesson

Maybe a Cold War bunker, the underground
       house built into the side of a hill—
only a staircase roof, single gable, and
       shingled pitch. A cement floor—
marl, shale, and ore—a sliding glass door,

and gangly pine slope. In a ditch
       of goldenrod and aster, one could
drink from a mineral tap, an aquifer of silt
       and sand—miles from the Little
Miami. Springs of the Ohio River Valley

worn soft under the earth's pressure, and
       smooth as the Baldwin's keys. It filled
the length of the midcentury room, a baleen
       with water-worn skin, semi-glossed—
an unmoving pond's rim. Round its fluke

and fin: taut strings, red felt dampers,
       wooden hammers, and gold-plated
pins; the amber underside of its lid,
       agape like a raven's wing—
As ballet accompanist, the last

of the provincial professions, alongside
       farriers, shoe smiths, and piano tuners . . .
she'd arrive with canvas tote, dipping
       her head from side to side as her foot
grazed brass pedals, scuffed shoehorns,

heels hinged to floor, below L-shaped
        limbs. She'd pore over compositions,
publisher's proofs, notes fastened to staffs
        in sharp mathematical ink.
Confined, composed from the grief

of a son's too early death—
        Under the arc of a lamp, we'd sit,
Solfeggietto split across a stapled page, monophonic,
        a toccata in distinct sixteenths, when
the phone would ring. We'd jump

from bench and chair to chase—mid-lesson—
        cows back into their fence.
She'd demonstrate Chopin's *Prelude in B Minor*
        then Haydn's *Sonata in D Major*, the
Allegro con brio, as I followed her fingers

tripling below our chins. *Your turn,* she'd quip,
        and I'd take the barbed bars into
bare hands, heeling to windward, ballast
        and keel, its night sail, its halyard
spar, tussling worried lines by the bulb

of a lighthouse moon. Eventually she'd see
        the map, suggest a change of tack—we'd
compose our own—two pianists, one piano,
        upper and lower register, bow and stern,
buoyed tips gliding like skiffs over matte crests,

sharps and nuanced flats. I'd climb
        plywood steps, over eyeing knots,
to the gravelly earth, the trident-starred
        sky. No war here or even fear—only
placid dark, a porous air in the pitch of night.

Poem for the Gardener

It was consonance that brought him,
shovel in hand, thin grasp of wishbone
at his wrist. He unearthed the ground
at his sod-cusped feet and did not sing.

His boots were ripped at the top, black
rubber scraps where he had pulled them up
mornings in the dark, the kettle not yet
to a boil. The sweater he wore

was torn at mid-arm where it had caught
an oak branch—knitting loops and knots.
In the berry thickets looking for a bucket
he had left, his back would haul as with

a scythe, three miles from the sea. His speech
lurked quietly below his breath, brief spit
of under-loam. His lips were water-thin
and did not move when he spoke.

Sly magician, out of his sleeve such vegetation
he awoke, turning up as with a tuning fork,
turnips and onions and spuds, as he stood—
timbre and dance, on the hill slant.

In memory of Michael Thornton,
Kylemore Abbey gardener)

Rain in the Garden

A configuration of lettuce lined,
enthusiastic sprouts, in rows
of two, a lighter green than
a bad parsley leaf, a darker green

than celery. An interior measure,
in from the sea, the salty mist-tap
of rain, mistook for juice dripping
from the hard-skinned tongues

of apples. A ruddy, stone-poked path,
an elbow of sorts to walk on. The
gate hedge ahead, a rough sandpaper
stone with busted ledge and lip.

White plastic buckets, doubly riveted
at the top, without lids. In our hands,
their swinging silver lines tipping.
The pour and the pouring

for which there is no other word—
drenched, soaked, and soggy. A tree's
bulbed canopy. The stove in
its dim drum, the kettle exasperating.

Emily in Her Conservatory

I send you inland buttercups as out-door flowers are at sea.

—E.D. to Sarah Tuckerman

Through Oleander and Oxalis, her auburn chestnut hair, dark pink
      pinwheels, light pink stars, lavender bells. The "Spice Isles,"

she wrote, just beyond the Homestead's library. Emily in the
      Tropics, a worsted shawl over a fiddle-back chair,

a plat of low-lying Geraniums, purple Heliotropes, her sloping
      shoulder by a shelf of soil-dusted bulbs bulging above

their brief expanse of earth like Cypress knees. Fringed Gentians,
      the sweet lemon scent of Daphnes, red Camellias; a white

Jasmine from Mr. Bowles. Her hands turning chalky clay-fired pots
      under thick waxy leaves. A soft hum in the warm enclosure,

frost on the south-facing pane, wood-smelling ferns in its humid
      center. She'll mail them, her inland emissaries, to meet

every anguish or ordinary hour. Black velvet ribbon around February
      bouquets. What summer her winter garden now makes—

until the June Delphinium breaks the horizon like a tall-masted
      ship, its bow wake unfurling, triumphant from the sea.

The Brass Orchard

A wall of four gardens separates us.
A bull by the East gate grazes there.
Even during wartime your father
did not eat the crust of his bread.

It's spawning season now. Fishermen
are clothed statues along the streamside.
Their waterproof attire matches ours.
The rain and the sea and the empty air

collapse here. We wait under an
apple tree. A rip of denim string
hangs from your apron. Quiet
and lean, the garden commences

another picking season. One spring
you hide a cow—too good to sell—
beyond the orchard gleam, when
the budget was low. (The others

would never know.) This year's cattle
are still out, a teeth-bitten pasture,
a broad ream of yellow—and a dearth
that has outstayed itself. I take your

father's heed in your death. And in
the stillness that turns the fruit of
loss into an alloy of tone collect one
horn note and one apple sapling's

rose. Though tampered by grief
they resound from their brass mute
a muse, a thousand leaf-graced
merriments of its orcharding.

Afternoon Tea

It's three o'clock, time
for tea, time to come home
now from the garden.

We prefer loose leaf, right
from the spoon to the
sizzle of the gray-white

kettle. Tedious, we stop, abrupt,
our fuss, pour the water on top
to a boil in our cup. We sip

without a word it seems
for hours, on our tongues
nothing in particular. Do take

another biscuit, tan flat crust
to fit its Christmas tin. Bran,
(poor dog, since gone), asleep

by the stove. Oh how the
windows steam over. The
damp drafts, O Lord, the rain.

The Fields

The hill is riveted by plod-slips where the sucklers
in their wild idle ambition tore down it at the sight
of an open gate, the stench of silage on the wind.

Now the wind is in, tearing the black sack tarp that
billows up, an immense whale-rip in its side, the entire
length of winter. Tires, deflated weight, are thrown

with a hoist on top. Rusted and rough, the old gate
creaks, as it ought, shut. The holly extends behind it,
bright berries that gleam a solitary foliage, and what's

left of November. The bull swings, a trod slowing in,
in a cold air off the coast, rounding near the back. Steam
breathing imparts the rite of winter, the rain shelled

in ice, the complete frost-insistence forward, sustained
by hooves that bounce thick to the barnyard down. In
these months the bales flick open, splaying in their mercy.

Poem for Memory

for Rachel in St. Paul

I felt all bone, yet
I was clumsy as the flesh, fumbling
with such a preposterous rush—
I think I cannot be good.

I suppose even God was clumsy,
rushing with such love at the creation.
I poke and prod. There must be
some life left yet. Hurt is not

a refinable art. It is perpetually
raw. Not by accident have I
uncovered it. The wild poppy
of my heart pierced in its

red-black center pulses in rapid
succession, beating so abruptly
the yellow needles quiver at it
not knowing what to do.

And Her Herbarium

'most all girls are making one.

—Emily Dickinson, age 14

And in her herbarium, she displayed five types of *Ranunculus:*
Creeping Buttercup, Early Buttercup, Hispid Buttercup,
Bulbous Buttercup, Tall Buttercup. In a separate, smaller

collection were twenty-two specimens mounted within
a sewn squire of twelve leaves, another nineteen sheets
with specimens from the Middle East. As for the sixty-six

sheets of the main album, its preservation proved difficult,
the curator notes. One by one the insect-damaged fragments
had to be kept in envelopes affixed with wheat-starch paste

(*Paste*—surely E. would approve). She collected Geranium after
Geranium, Violets, and Narcissus, labeling each with meticulously
small cursive below upright stems, or stems folded under stems

with veiny grasshopper angles. The large muted-yellow
Cactus flower takes half a page. She'd confuse modern-day
botanists by attaching to a specimen name its color in Latin:

Verbascum alba (i.e., *Verbascum blattaria*). She misidentified Poison Ivy
as Bittersweet (but so too Thoreau, notes the astute curator, mistook
the viny foliage for Silver Maple); and the Closed Gentian—the one

with a parched Corolla, that Purple Creature who tried to be a Rose—
as Thistle. But who could fault young Emily—who, after all, was like
'*most all girls*—for misspelling "Petunia" as "Patunia"? Arranged

sheet after sheet in "silent rank," pressed petal to emerald curve
of leaf, with a "Despatch of pink"—in good will seem to say
though they cannot speak—"Mistress is 'not at home'"—

Now Horses

Kylemore Abbey, Co. Galway, Ireland

When the white tour bus with square black windows
stops along the one-lane road, we are far beyond the
coiffed hedges, hidden in the brambles, our backs

bent over thick blackberries. "They like to see a nun
and a young girl in red overalls," she says. If someone
approaches, she'll pretend she doesn't hear, let me

talk, I the quieter one of the two. What does it mean—
now that she is gone, and the fields have carried on.
Now horses graze where she had kept her Charolais.

The earth hoof-tilled in the muddy months by four-
legged beasts, through each dew and each frost.
She must be in the farm kitchen, near the table,

near the worn-down chair, or in the gray dappled
coats of the Connemara ponies, muscles twitching
as if touched by a hand that is not there—

an architectured but pliant anatomy they inhabit,
forelocks brushed aside in the Atlantic air. There
she would be and not down the lane in the cemetery

under a cross placed in sparkling rocks. Not at
the far static end of the skyward-pointing gables
of the Gothic chapel but in the mottled light of its

windowed tracery, adrift in the angled corners cobbed
with dust, along the path of its flying buttresses to
where I think of her standing beside me under a

tree's wide canopy, sheltering us from an October
downpour one leaf-worn afternoon. But as soon
as it begins it will stop, and we'll emerge from wet

hedgerows heavy with light. "Now then," she'll
say, and we'll move on to the next thing. For a time,
we'll forget life's brevity, the narrow streams that

ran down our oversized raincoats while side by
side in stillness we watched, Wellingtons lined up,
two figures like horses waiting out the rain.

Sleepy Tom

Sleepy Tom, a pacer who set a world's record of
2:12 1/4 at Chicago, July 25, 1879, was foaled in the
schoolhouse yard on North Main Street in Bellbrook.

—Sugarcreek Township, Ohio

What was it about Sleepy Tom, lathered
in froth, his flank chalk-lined with sweat.
He was driven into the Little Miami River,

as the village lore goes, hot off the bottom track
after a nag race. Sold—bought for $7.50
and a jug of whiskey. He soon went blind

from heat stroke and the sudden change in
temperature but ran the Grand Circuit—
Louisville, Columbus, Cincinnati—

pulling a high-wheeled sulky behind. And
in Chicago he'd set the world record, come
to be known—a hundred years later—to the

town historian, and to us schoolchildren. Ghost
horse at the schoolyard's edge at the edge of town.
The headless horseman's lost horse. The horse

outside the classroom window. Grazing
through first grade, second grade. In third
grade his lithe contour accompanied

a lone oak, shadowed dyad in silhouette
visible from a school bus pane. Was it that
he ran, his *élan vital* propelling us both

toward some future form that made me
pay attention? Made me look for him in
every unplowed field, on each slick-paged

textbook, at the perimeter of every day? I took
comfort that he'd recognize the flat leather
straps, dull clips of sand against steel toes,

sulky spokes whisking alongside fetlocks,
brisk air rounding his pink-flared nostril
above his warm muzzle, metal bit on tongue—

On the same stretch of track, now road,
along a curve in the same river, I'd ride
another horse through bent trees and

bank rock, incognizant and blind at fourteen
to depthless rapids or the bottomless run. Barrel
deep, she'd plunge, her thick neck rising up

and down, evenly, like a musical measure.
Her forelegs seesawed in a high march, as if
buoyed on a carousel at a county fair.

She'd know what to do—did not spook,
without the surety of earth staying her
loosened hooves. She'd carry me, like

my first horse, through currents and cold
undercurrents, then hoist us both onto the bank,
shaking the water off her unquestioning back.

Emily and Sue

One Sister have I in our house —
And one a hedge away.
                    Emilie

                    —E.D. to Susan Huntington Dickinson

A *hedge away* the Evergreens and Sue—
            and from and to the Homestead
                        an uneven grass-edged path,

an antiquated August lawn, a forenoon sun.
            Dear Sue—writes Emilie, baking bread—
                        sleeves rolled, milk poured

in Indian and Rye. *Perhaps this verse would suit you better*—
            dough in oven, flour on brow. She'll lay
                        the loaf—round, domed, and brown—

Just a crumb—in a basket on her arm. To her
            garden she'll ask, Who would like to join—?
                        Hollyhocks, front-buttoned

and fresh—*To Carry in the Hand.* From her dress
            she'll unpin her poem into Sue's warm
                        palm, Hibiscus on a dash—

The Sick Calf

The sick calf lies limp on his side with
a small black chin cupped in my curved hand.

His eyes are half-closed in a watery haze,
his hoofed legs bent and staked apart like

awning poles to prop him up, as if detached
from his Holstein frame. His back hips

are boned elbow joints jarring out from him
two slim javelins hurled in a lolling arch.

His body, himself a scythe—has slipped from a
thrown hand in the air. Split wheat strands scatter

inside his pneumonic lungs, poking the sponge
that squeezes a foamy cough with each breath—

I wait for a spear to angle barnward and
pierce his heart, or for some farmer to come

pull him back, dragging the dead weight out
where the Earth on its pointed axis turns.

Night

I've given in to the cow's fierce lowing,
opened the door to let her in. It's night
anyhow, even the dark gets lonely
for her sleeping calf. Love, dark

and dust-webbed, step in the straw bed
comb, milk the honey from a lick of tongue.
Fresh dung, sac of birth, the tick of trough pump
watering out thirst. Everything desirous in its mess.

Milkweed

From the ditches
they'd sprout, like any other
flower, fertile in their floss
and fervid

in their kind regard
for milk cooling in an August
thicket. Nearby a cow edges
in her heft and graze,

summering in her cud.
The morning's beams on green
crabgrass pastures slip past
the wet maneuverings

of a tractor blade. Bikes
deserted at the quick turn of kickstands
collapse from where we have come
gutting the silk-lined pods—

merciless in our love. How we'd
burrow out the glued cotton tufts
seared to their scablike seams. Now
lambs' ear husks

hollowed and propped
upon stems like chaff in November
like low-perching chickadees
in spring. Like

aged hands upon limbs,
their bent wrists reaching above
the roadside. It was not unlike
diving to the lake bottom

in July and snatching
the empty mollusks, the ones
other shells would cling to—
    their slick cataract

    coverings basking
in sun water, one on top of
another. Why we'd exhume
    them one by one,

    then place them
on the white-washed pier
in rows and did not give them
    back their lives.

Oxheart

for Howard Schubiner, MD

> "It's all in your mind" is almost insulting, implying
> there's something strange or weak about you or that
> the symptoms are in your imagination. This is most
> unfortunate, since the symptoms are very real, the
> result of a very physical process.
>
> — John Sarno, *The Divided Mind*

Taut elastic tomato, sweet heirloom from
a grandparent's garden. Oxheart—whorled
and bulbous, not as acidic, bladder shaped—
now round inflamed planet: *Interstitial Cystitis*—
a condition common in cats. The urologist taps

the end of his pen: "Looks like we've ruled out
all the bad stuff."—I consult my vet—
try Glucosamine Chondroitin. Amitriptyline.
Cystoscopy with Hydrodistension. An alkaline
diet. Take aloe vera. Buy an aloe vera

plant as symbol. Take a turn of mind—
Tension Myositis Syndrome. The neurology
of pain, of chronic perception. From
cortical regions the brain fires off signals—
Are you there? the body, earnest follower,

answers, *I'm here, I'm here*—a conditioned
response. *Like Pavlov's dogs!* the kind doctor says.
I step into the neural fray. Drink coffee, spoon
spaghetti sauce from a jar—*You will get better.*
I see this just about every day—I run out into

the garden where my husband, the scientist,
turns compost. It is early spring. His measured
reply—*We'll see*—makes me question his belief.
Yet mine, already rooted in August—Oxheart,
the sweat of the earth, an organ of earth.

Emily and Katie

> The world is not acquainted with us.
>
> —E.D. to Catherine Scott Turner, circa March 1859

The Dartmouth ophthalmologist must measure
      the newly discovered 1859 daguerreotype
against the one from twelve years prior, comparing

eye socket to eye socket, among other anatomies
      and asymmetries, age progression, the
distance from iris edge to lower lid; the length

of upper lid from crease. In both, the left lower
      lid sits lower than the right; the right eye
opening is slightly larger than the left. But Emily,

I'd recognize you anywhere. The same year you
      send Catherine a poem: *When Katie walks,*
this simple pair accompany her side. I'd recognize you

not just in 21st-century Amherst by your white dress—
      (though in 1859 you aren't wearing it yet)—not
only in your garden, cleaning up after the Hollyhocks

who leave their clothes around—or in my garden—in
      the late-blooming gentian, two butterflies
going out at noon. *When Katie runs unwearied they follow*

on the road. But since the scientists require proof
      by hypothesis, they measure—is it *you?*—
(indeed the Dartmouth ophthalmologist concludes

you are *you*—). Besides those *look* like your shoulders;
      those are *your* fingers on your lap. And
When Katie kneels, their loving hands clasp her pious knee.

Again, as in 1847, you've crossed a laced ribbon
            around your neck, your bold hair has the
same cowlick part; that's your brow line to nose—

though you no longer sit alone: the archivists note
            Catherine beside you in widows' black, examine
the fabric of your out-of-fashion blue check dress—

but what really gives you away is not any
            reproducible experiment or matched
stitch—but yes, your own knowing, laughing?

light-glinting eyes—*Ah Katie! Smile at Fortune, with
            two so knit to thee*—peering at me as I peer
at you—your left arm extending, to a Katie too.

On Seeing Andrew Wyeth's *The Berry Picker* at Age Seven

Had she fallen asleep after harvesting the day's berries,
her clasped fingertips having formed domed blisters like
the supple blue pearls with their calyx star tops? Their thin
branches had broken off with her indiscriminating pinch
then left their sepal's jagged shadow. Compiled, no, *tossed*
in their cedar-bark baskets, they continually permeate the
sweet soft wood smell of earth, a June among the timothy,
the white-clumped aster. I think she died there on that hill,
forever among the sleeping dead, slanted but unslipping,
her bare feet no longer in need of shoes, her face, a hat—
her shirt, just a breeze in the linen sadness that is her breath.

American History Primer

The apple is to America as the potato is to Ireland or the olive
to Italy. "The apple," as Virginia pomologist James Fitz proudly
proclaimed in 1872, "is our democratic fruit."

—Peter J. Hatch, Monticello Gardens and Grounds

At Monticello, in his fruit garden, Jefferson
grew a variety of cultivars—Hewes' Crab or
Taliaferro, for cider. Albemarle Pippin
or Esopus Spitzenburg for a tabletop display.

There were other faces, other names
unmentioned among the gallery of stern,
white-browed statesmen from a third grade
history lesson. We recited the Pledge

of Allegiance, and learned why
the Statue of Liberty stood, her tired arm
with chipping copper torch. And to the words,
which were her words—Emma Lazarus—

pundits applied, then as now, more statement
than inquiry. Despite her silent-lipped cry
against human possession: Chinese immigrant
or African kingdom. In the fall we rode stout

school buses to a nearby orchard; engines
hurled with such heft through Tecumseh's
Ohio countryside I thought my chest would
split like a fibrous wood. A lull then surge—

Reagan on the radio. All tires and exhaust. An
allotment of schoolchildren in trees grasping
hands through leave-sieved light, to pluck—
democratic or not, the distinctly American fruit.

Picture in a Pandemic

for Matt Metzler, and for Finn

Still young enough to hold my hand,
it might be the last year his supple-
boned body, tepid fledgling, buries

behind my leg like a wren's barred wing.
Its primary import has always been shield.
He wears a cotton ear-strap mask, navy

shorts; on his shirt, T-Rex this year—
We maneuver past the elder class
having a socially distanced snack. From

his eye I see a riveted tree trunk, stout,
sanguine, tower from its hem of play-
worn dirt, turret or spire or minaret—

Above the folded grass, his shoes,
lithe, jet-black. His hair is half-cut,
I cut his ear—narrowest blade edge

biding there. He shifts his legs forward,
a British Grenadier, to the photographer's
prompts and cues. Against the oak,

with verdant pose and without guise,
he looks past both lens and scope—
only then can consciousness

take its brief transit across the late
morning light. Last winter when
he bolstered his staunch reproach, hid

under a desk, his teacher did not force
with speech but knew silence to be
language enough to stay fear's foothold

in a usurped land. Silence gives space,
protection. Though we know it goes
both ways. Here, a sturdy bulwark—

his teacher a stalwart. They stand
at the helm, loud as the most
raucous fight, or birds taking flight.

Seeing the Deer

Where we met three deer
traversed there, sudden
like a night scare. Their gray,
stemmed hooves split

the leafless thin woods
into a crack which transfixed
the sky and land and trees
into a dance so quick

they were gone—
kindling to a spark. What
warmth they gave
the cold January morning,

their large hearts beating
under hide and flesh, the wind
sweeping white across the hills.
We stood so still then. And the quiet,

the quiet. Down the road we knew
the monks bowed and kneeled
in black robes. Their gentleness had
encompassed us, separate kindred

as we came and left, for years,
in that kind sanctuary
made holy. When does
a placid acceptance begin

to love the body in its slow
terror of the deep earth's keeping?
Love, so quiet, has no rib
to contain the dark heart of it. Yet

it chooses to live in the body
without abandonment. Ethereal
in its boundlessness, what love
could resist such love?

(for Rose)

Her Cricket

Further than birds in the low August sun
        is the cricket corpse she enclosed with a poem,
its "spectral Canticle," its unobtrusive repose. Little
        druid in a furrow of lines. Winged-thorax—
nature's preface—its remittance postponed. But for
        a gradual grace undersigned with a title:
"My Cricket"—she sent to Mabel, if only to say
        it *was* (and she rarely titled poems)—
no celestial ordinance nor other claim disclose
        the sum of its Autumn countenance now.

        (after E.D.'s "Further in Summer than the Birds")

Poetry Cloak

She covets hens like couture shoes.
      They step around her King Louis
heels and into her house. She tells me

their lineage: Rhode Island Red,
      Plymouth Rock, ISA Brown.
About her kitchen they cluck

under the half-light of morning. Daft
      the chickens are and operose,
with their oil-preened feathers,

auburn hackles, and trifold feet. Outside
      they scrape the earth back
with theatrical finesse, shift

mechanical heads in abrupt,
      unceremonious angles. Among
the flora, a cloak—bought in

a Lake Michigan tourist town, and
      shared between—the shade of
the ISA Brown, botah on bodice and

sleeves: coral thread, copper stitch,
      and mahogany swatch. Vintage,
Victorian; a Persian tapestry with

faux fur cuffs. The hens are only remotely
      aware, or temporarily so, of
a similarly hued fox, a trotting memory,

far-off, head down, its white tussock tail
        skirting a timber-trussed coop
and straw-bed clutch. Over decades,

we held readings in attics. Bulbs then herbs
        planted in backyard gardens.
A pair of French empire armchairs

pulled close for tea. *Collected Letters*, of whom?
        purchased at a musty antique store,
among familial yet unaffiliated heirlooms,

handiwork brought from the dead. A
        wrought iron candelabra painted
white for Dickinson's 168th birthday,

her poems we read behind a wooden door
        as she had done; wax-drip candles, pastel
confetti—paper ash on a hardwood floor.

Years, mere carriers, fleets or flocks, and round
        like clocks, trunk rings, figs we tasted
one summer evening from a neighbor's tree.

Lightly with Occasion for Beauty

Lightly with occasion for beauty
the leaves overturn what had haunted them
all summer. Haunted them in that green
ripening silkworms devour in, the hot
sunlight woven thick from a dew-

splintered wood. How my eyes squinted
in it, looking up, as if in perpetual
childhood, bewildered as the half-spun
gaze of partial love, or the possibility
of love, unrecognizable, or as far back.

The Master Letters

Letter One (Spring 1858)—*blue-ruled, not embossed,*
      folded into quarters; a drop of ink mars the third page.
"Master, I am Ill—" writes Emily, "but grieving more

that you are ill." But she'll use her stronger hand,
      violets at her side, robins near. The messages
to him her disobedient flowers did not convey. She'll

count the Sabbaths at sea until they meet on shore—
      "will the or whether the hills will look as blue"
as "sailors say—" Letter Two (early 1861)—*gilt-edged,*

lightly ruled, embossed, in pencil. "Oh—did I offend it—"
      "~~Didn't it want me to tell it the truth~~," the letter
begins, without salutation. *This* Daisy "only asks—a task—"

"something to do" for her Preceptor—Samuel Bowles, Rev.
      Wadsworth, Judge Lord (—Higginson?)—she does
not or will not say—a "love so big it scares" her but the

tomahawk in her side does not hurt—"~~If you~~ Her Master
      stabs her more." Letter Three (Summer 1861)—
blue rule, embossed; within a decorative frame, a queen's head. "If

you saw a bullet hit a Bird"—the bird, unshot, would
      tell the shooter as much. Though he doubt—
"One drop more from the gash that stains" his Daisy's

bosom, would he then "<u>believe</u>?" "Daisy confessed"—
      "Pompeii heard" then "hid forever." Could he
"come to New England ~~this summer~~?" "~~Could~~ Would"

he come "To Amherst?" To walk with Carlo for
      "an hour—" "~~Would it do harm?~~" "~~Will you~~
~~tell me if you will?~~" "Would you like to"—"Master?"

Gaudium et Dolor

Next will be daffodils at the edge of snow. Bright yellow,
and first color of spring. One boyhood winter in Michigan
he dislocated his arm: *Red Rover Red Rover, send Robert right over!*
when off he ran, jumping over the schoolboy-linked barricade,
one classmate's weight bearing down. The next year—1938, '39?—
in the yard, frozen earth all around, the same classmate pitched
a baseball, hitting his elbow back into place. *The coincidence!*
he'd exclaim. That's how it was. Joy not pain. This distant
February sunlight moving across the room. The same light
hovered on the casket before it was lowered into the ground,
holding us all a while longer on this earth.

i.m. Robert A. Boehmer
(August 13, 1931 – November 25, 2021)

Reverie

In her saddle she will carry him
when I cannot. Then she will carry him,
beast of his burden, her wooden hooves rent
from the paddock's rigid terrain, under his pointed
elbows, her quiescent dust. Summer afternoons, they drift—
brown skiff on green pastures. Her wither crest and backbone's
pitch. Her neck's an answered question his helmet tilts upon.
Though they stand they gallop through a field of purple clover.
They gallop far circles, strewn ellipses, mere thread, the
black leather discus on which he rides, the sky's pupil
absorbing light and trees and clouds and at a pinpoint,
a mother, squinting just out of their periphery.

Mythological Horses

for Amy Sturm

> Tangible horses, tangible texts—
>
> —Vicki Hearne, "Ana Halach Dodeach"

At first in death horses will defy this expectation; then as *their heads
lengthen*, their mythical spirits will form from a thousand brushings,
and as bristles stroke up dust, they'll stir the winged Balius and

Xanthos and the unwinged Arion at Achilles's calloused heel.
And from the sea four Hippocamps will slough off Poseidon's
blue chariot. The mares of Diomedes will feed on human flesh.

No one forgets Zeus's flying Pegasus. But what about Helios's
fire-breathing steeds? He'll release them from their sun stable
and allow them their own pace. But these *a priori horses are not

real horses.* No coffin bone sinks their loping step. *The frightened
horses forget the veracities of haute école* (a mere derivative of mythical
forms). And the *actual horse* hesitates at the aberrant light refracted

on a pasture gate. These horses are not *lamed by foolish perfections
of flight* but by the shift and spook of thinly blooded ligaments,
flying lead changes notwithstanding, a nervous muscle's impulse

with *a dozen false starts.* The sorrel gelding is secure only in
the ground's low-humming against his earth-shorn chin,
his teeth a fulcrum levering grass from its intractable roots,

mythical only to a young girl's vined branch, a horizontal
berth to take his ghostly shape. From withers to croup the dip
of his back shadowed in the paddock sun might be the sway

of a dropped wing. But flies congregate in the black-lipped
corners of Pegasus's eyes. And though a thousand stirrings
will startle, he'll stamp a tangible hoof into tangible text.

Eros

I run from him like I ran
the paths of my girlhood,
whipping past all the old trees
who stand for proof

that I was there—
if I look up, he is sure
to vanish
as if stumbling upon a buck

in the wholly empty forest.
If I speak my voice is grass.
I could live and not
love, but what grief would I

spare? The only boy I spoke to
as a girl?—Stephen—
I am not seven, although my slow
womanhood races there.

Ghost Apple

I had thought the home devised the life,
       the unseen rafters above daily
affairs, joists spanning years. Remote

from that house and where other people
       now live. I had thought the years
into days could reassemble. But found

otherwise. February's rain, frozen,
       encapsulated an October-ripe apple—
bruised like a knee on a summer's day. Fruit

in metamorphosis and by the weight of
       its core slipped through the ice dome
of its likeness. Into the open air—

mere passage, or possibly voyage. Above
       not one but several apple-shaped
bulbs hollowed and held by chandeliered

branches as if on a snow-globed tree
       in a childhood orchard. Upturned,
through swirling white flakes emerge:

wooden ladder, rung; fall fescue at
       its edge, and a brother beside. Was it
the body that was lighter or the mind?

"Master, Let Me Lead You"

> All men say "What" to me, but I thought it a Fashion—
>
> —E.D. to Thomas Wentworth Higginson

"You think my gait 'spasmodic'—I am in danger, Sir—"
    Dickinson wrote to Higginson in June 1862. Like

her, he'd consider fall flowers, winter birds; nature, an
    unfeigned corroborator. She had just her lexicon

for companion, and a "terror since September."
    "The 'hand you stretch me in the Dark,'" she

had told him, "I put mine in." Of her verse she'd ask, "But
    will you be my Preceptor, Mr Higginson?" (after her

death, he would confess he was not—). But by August he'd
    leave Boston for South Carolina as Colonel Higginson,

commander of the first Union regiment of freed slaves. Eight
    years later when he finally stood in the dim parlor:

"These are my introduction," she'd say, placing two
    day-lilies in his hand. And she had placed his books,

Out-door Papers, Malbone, on the table. Baffled, bewildered yet
    pulled by her nervous timbre, he was not just editor

but friend (and she asked much of friends). She was so exhausting,
    he'd write to others, "I am glad not to live near her."

(And they met just twice.) But he did not say "What" to her—
    How different they were, or how different she was.

Higginson: *Voices of birds, hushed first by noon . . . begin once more, . . . on infinite melodies of a June afternoon.* Dickinson:

"The birds begun at Four o'clock — Their period for Dawn — A music numerous as space — But neighboring as Noon —"

No wonder he thought her gait spasmodic. "You only shroud yourself in this fiery mist and I cannot reach you," he'd

write. And Emily, with acquainted step: "The Wildnerness is new—to you. Master, let me lead you"—from plank to

plank she'll first go—a pair of wild violets in her blue net shawl, plain white piqué, a fluttering of birds aflame in the firmament.

Night Eye

White gravel in the height of an August sun.
I'd swung a lead rope, looking for the mare
who'd jumped the fence. My father, not a horseman

nor a farmer, drove off in his black VW Beetle
after her. Half thoroughbred, she'd race for miles
along country roads before stopping to graze

at the edge of a field. In the fall, I'd ride through
wooded hills, pulling knees to chest, on paths lined
by furrowed oak bark. In winter, she'd rear against

the black skeletons of summer, and a hawk behind
a clump of straggling brown leaves. I'd rise
and fall with her, as if by nature she were bipedal,

breaching the sky like some water-breathing creature
to air. She already knew how to leave the earth, to
return to earth, the suspension bounding her ligaments

on both sides. Later, in the dim barn, her ears perched
like watchful sparrows among the hay. Her ardent stare,
her domestic sigh. From the spring mud she'd emerge

wearing a prehistoric coat of armor, belying a vestigial toe—
gnarled chestnut, the night eye—evolved from some ancient
forest-dwelling Equus. Under the March moon I'd call then hear

a hollow drumming. The world is muscle is music. The chill
air, her warm breath. She'd nuzzle my side with her fingerlike
lip as if it were not Adam's but a horse's rib inside me.

Bon Secours

There it was, the farm kitchen,
where we had steeped our tea,
the iron stove—stoic like

a Mother Abbess at the back
of a chapel. The kettle,
a third guest at our table.

"Kindly get off the fence!"
you'd admonish—
schoolgirls in wool gray

skirts, navy socks pulled up
to knees, sweaters with gold
medallion patch. They'd slip

off the horizontal slats
in a flutter like startled geese
to water, heads on diagonal,

adolescent eyes askance.
We'd pick blackberries
and black currants in an

afternoon opening in
October, fill buckets with
lettuce with an importance

only the earth took notice.
Your mottled hands, your
widow's peak. We'd step

across angled vestiges
of glasshouses, shards of
geometry and light, where

a black and white cat napped.
Over years you'd write in wiry-
vined script—of cows going out

and coming in, which sisters
had died—how you'd become
redundant in the garden. When

I arrived the abbess pressed
her palms in a locketlike clasp:
In hospital. Bon Secours. Galway.

A persistent cough, a
congested heart. The way
back was long. The smells

removed of bells and bustle.
The deserted choir stalls,
the wooden stair. In hospital,

your pinned veil lies limp
above the register, belt loose
along the sill. You look up

from your newspaper as if
no years had passed. As if
I walked in from another room.

At Cambridge as a young
barrister you wore a feather
in your hat. That's also how

I see you: walking swiftly
across a crowded street. Life
still before you. When I leave

you try to stand, inches shorter.
On the floor, my son at three
plays at your feet: "Pussy cat,

Pussy cat, where have you been?"
—and you answer him—"I've been
to London to visit the Queen."

Virgil's Font

Despite the teacher's repeated promptings
he refuses to write in lower case but instead
forms rigid Roman capitals, like Virgil's,
scored from a thumb-grasped pencil grip.

His chisel's a quill, his quill a graphite tip. At
night he is thankful, he says, for opposable
thumbs. Opposable, he puts his foot down.
He simply won't heel to a medieval monk's

hasty minuscules worn down in the dim
Scriptorium. His Ticonderoga jibes grand
majuscules like Aeneas's Sicily-bound
ships. His vessel's a fleet, his fleet adrift.

Their bows rise and fall across the dashed
lines of his composition book. It is Palinurus
sleeping at a paper helm. His pitch pine tar,
a rudderless hull. He brushes eraser dust like

calloused skin from a pumice stone. Yet still
he fastens his bent gaze from Carthage toward
Lavinium. Down the page his lead-gray As
spire out like sails from a ruled horizon.

By the Pier, an Island

The turtles' forsythia-stroked necks: each a stout inch—
gnarled bark or dried fig. Lake dross onshore reminiscent
of an ocean, this far inland. Their hardscape shells, a carapace,
an olive with pimiento-skirted lip, a pie's crimped edge. Against
the puddied plastron, our thumb and index grip, claw-caught

skin, a needle's poke, a stippling's pinch. With
a cataract splash—our sunstruck arms outstretched—
they scurried in. What did we seem to them? Part landscape
part interior, all summer underfoot from underwater mirrors
of ferned chlorophyll, mantis-green fronds propped in tea water—
wrists wafting in conversation, a conductor's plied semaphore
against the aluminum boat's agitated rope, its sidelong slip.

Varicella Zoster

(chicken pox, shingles)

Here you are again. How old we have both become
since we first met; a trip to Greenfield Village in Detroit,
cut short from a brother's sudden pox on arms, on chest.

Then my own. Lighter then, *varicella zoster,* we've grown
in pain. So why am I comforted by you, some ill-worn
anguish, or a path to my younger self, from her to me—

back home in Ohio, crossed-legged on the living room
floor in morning light, same sun. These same hands,
veins upraised, pulled a hairbrush through also lighter

hair, bristles like barbs stoking miniature volcanoes
against my scalp, blue floral nightgown stretched tight
between knees. Like you, *varicella zoster,* lying dormant

all this time, through all the diversions and departures
of life. Awakened now, her age-old rash erupting on my
back—I keep asking her, Does it itch or does it sting?

Hearth

for Kelley Beeson

July filled the tree-lined street in a glass-domed nursery
        of staggered greens and reds and pinks: spirea,
weigela, and azalea among boxwoods packed so tightly

it was hard to find you—framed on a wooden porch.
        A block away, the cement curb tripped my step;
I waved my arms. The last time in an airport, before 9/11

and TSA checkpoints, I ran alongside you from gate to gate—
        to meet over your 10-minute layover in my town.
Those early brief emails to confirm each other's whereabouts

were like distant sightings on separate ships as we moved
        through life. If it were a hundred years ago or more
we'd only send paper letters in paper envelopes, slip poems

inside rounded creases like Dickinson—subtle, unspoken
        ridges we'd travel. We'd see our individual scripts,
inked chirography, in black, where calloused fingers pressed.

What I hold you'd soon hold too, the saw-edged stamp, a badge—
        circled and complete by its postmarked date. Now
we toss immediate type into invisible airways, a swift interior

door opening, a spirit without form. Do we need the option
        of destruction to not be destroyed? The tight-chest
silence of that September without planes, the absence of

the under-whir our ears had been accustomed to. Inside
        you've stacked your fireplace with books of poems—
authorless and titleless with unseen spines, horizonal

foredges forming clenched paper smiles, puzzled lines;
       on the surround: forest-green tiles like game
piece pawns, chalky grout. In the flue, on the hearth,

warmth's intrinsic laughter. Page to fire to plume—
       it could all go up in flame. But for now we
visit—cap, crown, and flashing—all smoke and poetry.

Called Back

Emily Dickinson, December 10, 1830 – May 15, 1886

> Sweet hours have perished here.
>
> —Emily Dickinson

The white coffin, the white ribbon—
carried out the Homestead's back door
        around her flowering garden, along
a spring grass footpath through the damp barn
        through a field of yellow buttercups.

After the afternoon fell and an evening beam
trod across her rose papered wall, her
        blush plum paisley stole. After a world
dropped down and down and an air above her
        bed stood still. And Austin and Lavinia

and Susan there—and the late daffodils and
the punctual may-flowers, silent. Just how then
        did her shape rise? In the dimming bustle
by an oil-lit lamp, wet cloth on her brow,
        a light-bristled brush, a metal comb—

her unchanged chestnut hair. Sue washing
her body robed in white—blue violets and
        one pink cypripedium on her neck
where breath had been. Vinnie placing two
        heliotropes near her hand. Sparrows

next will follow, a scattering of pine—an
anemone, and robins, bold and fluttering, will
        with her go—on an almost-summer day—
a wild violet lens, a vital stir between her and her
        bough-lined grave—an old bravery then—

Off Season

> Life separates us.
>
> —Truman Capote, *A Christmas Memory*

Toward each other we walk. You in a light yellow
        dress shirt, black trousers. I am nineteen,
maybe twenty, at a stately college in Ohio.

From inside three decades and the blurred periphery
        of memory you visit me. In Connemara,
between the Twelve Bens, along the heath, among

the heather—you turn on the worn gravel
        to say goodbye. Ireland in October:
for you the off season is always better, fewer

people, different weather. Last summer
        I jumped out of your car—always
terrible at goodbyes (and now to you I travel),

the always leaving, the anticipation of leaving.
        Twelve years it had been. When I
first saw you I saw your hair, white like

a river birch, like Michigan snow those many
        years ago, plowed drifts along packed
roads, thick inches on thin branches. There are

measures that defy time, like your voice, or my
        homesick-spun heart. Now fifty, I am
the age you were then. You reached your hands

to me. Now to you I reach—you who are
        almost eighty. We outgrow our bodies.
And then? And then in that other light meet.

Of Thomas Merton

for Kymberly Taylor

> Tall oaks from little acorns grow.
>
> —14th-century proverb

We spoke of Thomas Merton along the Chesapeake—
        how your father had been a monk at Gethsemane;
surprisingly stern, Father Louis mostly kept to himself, he said—

when a branch we did not see fell. Its hollow weight opened
        the sky into airy silence. Then crow caws, trilling
cadences that for the eye was like light playing on knives.

*What can we gain by sailing to the moon if we are not able to cross
        the abyss that separates us from ourselves?* Merton wrote.
Perhaps we are co-conspirators to the Judas inside us,

wayward pilgrims in Dante's dark forest. Or perhaps our
        flickering lanterns will lead us to a living stream. And
from the bank we'll fix in each other's abyss a singular snail's

boat made of bark, on its bow lay moss as berm; and on
        a vertical stick tie a fern by its stem. Then with an oak's
acorn set out, first you, then me, our knees covered in leaves.

The Envelope Poems

On a mere brittle scrap that could just as easily
        be a modern-day discarded grocery list,
she writes—*I have no life but this*—then a space,

To lead it here—in a mix of cursive and block. In
        a yellowed isosceles triangle between brown
strips of torn adhesive: *How much—how little—is within*

our power, the word *power* bolstered in its vertex. Some are
        postmarked: AMHERST Nov. 9 MASS 1880
within a round black-inked stamp. Others have addressees:

Miss Lavinia Dickinson, below which in the bottom
        left-hand corner: *Care- Mr A. Dickinson, Esq.*;
still others: "Amherst House," affixed with U.S. postage:

George Washington's profiled bust with blue-green backdrop,
        a flag-striped blot; Three 3 Cents ribboned below
his stone chin, his powdered side curls inside an oval flower rim.

The monikers are ever Dickinson parlance, their roundhand
        ascenders and descenders looping and overturning—
Mr Edward Dickinson, Esq., Mrs Helen Hunt, Mr J. G. Holland—

along diagonal strokes. In a right angle triangle smaller
        than a Post-it Note, she has etched: *One note from*
One Bird   Is better than a million words, without a dash.

Nor any Death—she continues on the rectangular flap—
        lest dispelled from there—and on another:
perpendicular to her hairline name threaded through

a steel nib—*Miss Emily Dickinson*—she pencils in:
        To   light,   and
      then   return—

NOTES

"Thoreau's Sisters": Biographical information on the Thoreau family and italicized text are from Laura Dassow Walls's wonderful biography of Thoreau, *Henry David Thoreau: A Life* (Chicago: University of Chicago Press, 2017); and Kathy Fedorko's "Henry's Brilliant Sister," *New England Quarterly* 89:2 (June 2016): 222–56.

"Emily Dickinson's Lexicon": Italicized words, primarily nouns, verbs, adverbs, and adjectives, reflect entries found in the Emily Dickinson Lexicon, a database established by Brigham Young University, which can be found at https://edl.byu.edu/.

"And Her Herbarium": References to the herbarium's compilation are from Leslie A. Morris, foreword to *Emily Dickinson's Herbarium: A Facsimile Edition*, by Emily Dickinson (Cambridge: Belknap Press, 2006); and Ray Angelo, "Catalog of Plant Specimens," in Dickinson, *Emily Dickinson's Herbarium*. Poems referenced are 1424, 442, and 1520, respectively, from Dickinson, *Complete Poems of Emily Dickinson*, ed. Thomas H. Johnson (Boston: Little, Brown and Co., 1960).

"Emily and Sue": Italicized phrases are from Emily Dickinson, *Open Me Carefully: Emily Dickinson's Intimate Letters to Susan Huntington Dickinson,* ed. Ellen Louise Hart and Martha Nell Smith (Middletown, CT: Wesleyan University Press, 1998).

"Emily and Katie": The poem "When Katie walks" is from Emily Dickinson, *The Letters of Emily Dickinson*, ed. Thomas H. Johnson and Theodora Ward (Cambridge: Harvard University Press, 1958), letter 208. The epigraph is from letter 203. The italicized Hollyhock reference is from letter 771.

"Her Cricket": Dickinson sent the deceased cricket, along with her poem, "Further in Summer than the Birds," which she titled "My Cricket," to Mabel Loomis Todd. See Judith Farr, *The Gardens of Emily Dickinson* (Cambridge: Harvard University Press, 2004), 26.

"The Master Letters": Italicized words and Dickinson quotations are from R. W. Franklin, ed., *The Master Letters of Emily Dickinson*, by Emily Dickinson (Amherst, MA: Amherst College Press, 1986). Strike-through and underlined words reflect Dickinson's cancellations and emphasis as they appear in the facsimile reproductions. "Carlo" was Dickinson's beloved dog. It is unknown if final drafts of the letters were ever sent to their intended recipient(s). They portray a sometimes volatile and deeply personal Emily Dickinson, one not intended for the world to see.

"Mythological Horses": Italicized phrases are from Vicki Hearne's "Metaphysical Horse," "Every Time the Mountain," "A Country Scene," and "Riding a Nervous Horse," respectively. See Hearne, *Tricks of the Light: New and Selected Poems,* ed. John Hollander (Chicago: University of Chicago Press, 2007).

"Master, Let Me Lead You": Biographical content is from Brenda Wineapple, *White Heat: The Friendship of Emily Dickinson and Thomas Wentworth Higginson* (New York: Borzoi Books, A. Knopf, 2008); and Dickinson, *Letters* (Johnson and Ward, eds.), letters 265, 271, 342, 517. The italicized text is from T. W. Higginson, "My Out-Door Study," *The Atlantic* (September 1861), 302. The Dickinson poems referenced are 783, 876, 365 (*Collected Poems*, Johnson, ed.). Higginson describes Dickinson as wearing "a very plain and exquisitely clean white piqué and blue net worsted shawl" (Dickinson, *Letters,* letter 342).

"Called Back": The title refers to a letter Dickinson wrote to Louise and Fanny Norcross shortly before her death in May 1886: "Little Cousins, Called Back" (Dickinson, *Letters,* letter 1046). The epigraph is from poem 1767 (*Collected Poems*, Johnson, ed.) Poems alluded to are "I felt a Funeral, in my Brain," "I think just how my shape will rise—," "Where every bird is bold to go," "The Poet's light but Lamps," among others.

"Of Thomas Merton": The italicized passage is from Thomas Merton, *The Wisdom of the Desert* (New York: New Directions, 1960), 11.

"The Envelope Poems": Italicized passages are from Emily Dickinson, *Envelope Poems*, transcribed by Marta L. Werner and Jen Bervin (New York: Christine Burgin/New Directions, 2016). Dickinson recycled envelopes and scraps of envelopes as writing paper. All fifty-two envelope poems and writings appear in the full-color facsimile edition, Emily Dickinson, *The Gorgeous Nothings: The Envelope Poems of Emily Dickinson*, ed. Marta L. Werner and Jen Bervin (New York: New Directions, 2013).

ABOUT THE AUTHOR

KATIE LEHMAN received an MFA from the University of Notre Dame in 1999. While at Notre Dame, she was the recipient of the 1998 Billy Maich Academy of American Poets Prize, an award given to a Notre Dame student, graduate or undergraduate, for excellence in poetry. From 2004 to 2010, Lehman was assistant editor at the University of Notre Dame Press and for many years has served as a personal editor for her former teacher, the American poet, translator, and David Jones scholar John Matthias. She is the editor of Matthias's *Regrounding a Pilgrimage*, a collaboration with John Peck and Robert Archambeau (Dos Madres, 2018).